Building with Flexible Materials

Charmaine Robertson

Rosen REAL READERS

Rosen Classroom™
New York

Builders use many kinds of materials.

They can use metal, wood, plastic, and more.

Many buildings are made of flexible materials.

These materials can be bent to make different shapes.

Wood is a flexible material.
This skateboard ramp is made of wood.
See how it bends?

Plywood is a thin wooden board.
It has many layers.
It's strong but also flexible.

This canoe is made of wood.

It bends to give the canoe its shape.

The shape helps it float.

Steel is a strong metal.

It is made into thin sheets.

Car bodies are made of steel.

Aluminum can also be made into sheets.

It can be used to make parts of cars, planes, and buildings.

Plastic is a man-made material. It can be shaped into just about anything!

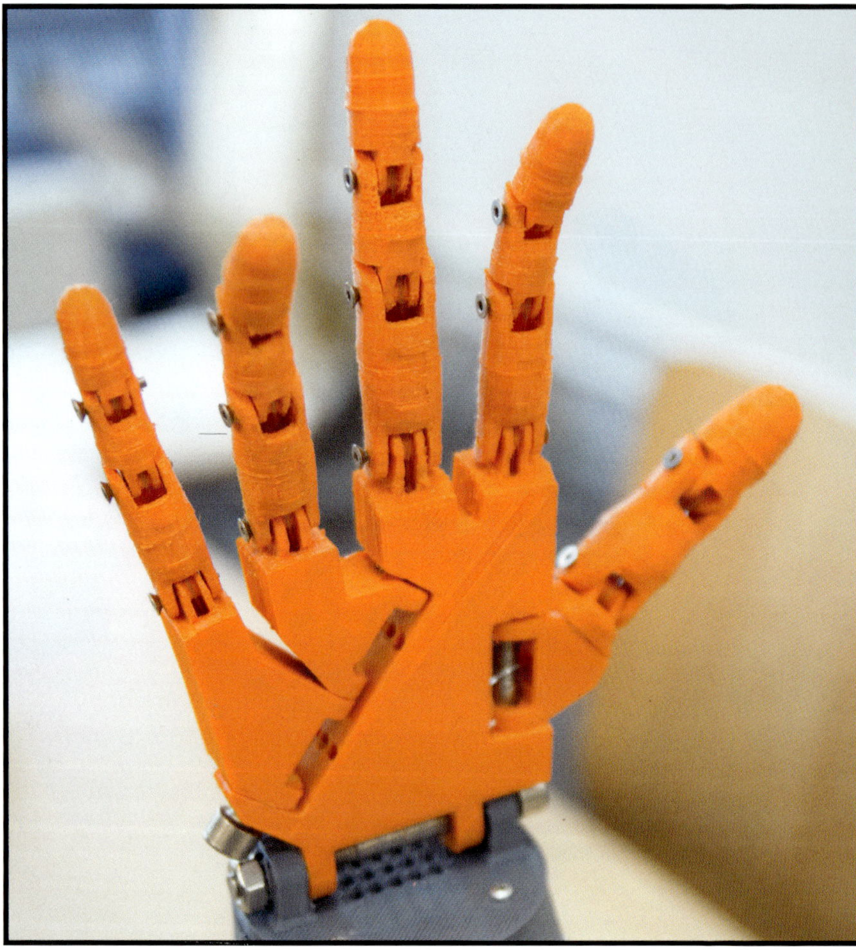

3-D printers can create many things out of plastic.

A 3-D printer made the plastic parts for this hand.

What will you build?

Which materials will you use?

Words to Know

aluminum

buildings

canoe

plastic

plywood

wood